Serenity

Finding Peace & Tranquillity

Written and compiled by
SARAH M. HUPP

Inspire Books is an imprint of Peter Pauper Press, Inc
Spire is a registered trademark of Peter Pauper Press, Inc

For photo credits and permissions,
please see the last pages of this book.

Designed by Heather Zschock

Copyright © 2003
Peter Pauper Press, Inc.
202 Mamaroneck Avenue
White Plains, NY 10601
ISBN 0-88088-254-9
Printed in China
7 6 5 4 3 2 1

Visit us at www.peterpauper.com

To:

From

Contents

Our Prayer for You

Serenity is found in the deliberate
adjustment of our lives to the will
of God. May you find this peaceful
blessing and a sense of God's
presence in the pages that follow.

S. M. H.

The Serenity Prayer

God, give us grace to accept with
serenity the things that cannot
be changed, courage to change
the things which should be changed,
and the wisdom to distinguish
the one from the other.

REINHOLD NIEBUHR

The LORD gives his
people strength;
The LORD blesses
them with peace.

PSALM 29:11, (NLT)

The Stillness
of Serenity

Great tranquility of heart
is his who cares for
neither praise nor blame.

THOMAS À KEMPIS

God is a tranquil being and
abides in a tranquil eternity.
So must your spirit become a
tranquil and clear little pool,
wherein the serene light
of God can be mirrored.

GERHARD TERSTEEGEN

And in His will is our peace.

DANTE ALIGHIERI

Contentment is
not the realization
of what you want,
but the recognition
of how much
you have.

He knows, He loves, He cares,
Nothing this truth can dim;
He does the very best for those,
Who leave the choice with Him.

WALTER B. KNIGHT

In Christ, we are relaxed
and at peace in the
midst of the confusions,
bewilderments, and perplexities
of this life. The storm rages,
but our hearts are at rest.
We have found peace—at last!

BILLY GRAHAM

There is Someone who cares
about us, who watches closely
for each individual: God!
Through him we can find rest
in spite of the catastrophes
that harass the world. He offers
us a place to stand, and hope,
even in an apparently lost world.
He offers a new beginning
to those of us who return to him.

GIEN KARSSEN

We waste a lot of energy
wishing for things we think
will bring us peace and serenity.
God has a better way.
Only by savoring each moment
and recognizing His hand in every
aspect of our lives can we find
the true serenity we crave.

A farmer visiting the city heard the noise of a cricket. A friend was amazed the farmer could hear the small noise amidst the city traffic. The farmer observed, "It all depends on what you're listening for."

With that, he dropped some
coins on the sidewalk.
Every head within a half block
turned toward the noise. . . .

What are you listening for?
Choose to hear peace.

Peace I leave with you;
my peace I give you.
I do not give to you
as the world gives.
Do not let your hearts
be troubled and
do not be afraid.

JOHN 14:27, NIV

When each earthly prop gives under,
And life seems a restless sea,
Are you then a God-kept wonder,
Satisfied and calm and free?

AUTHOR UNKNOWN

They who intentionally
interrupt the peace in which
they are living have not
hatred of peace, but only
wish it changed into a peace
that suits them better.

SAINT AUGUSTINE

It is in our best interest
to readily consent
to the will of God,
whate'er betide.
Therein lies the path
to peace, freedom, and
heartfelt joy.

The Grace of Acceptance

Let us take things as we find them.
Let us not attempt to distort
them into what they are not.
We cannot make facts. All our
wishing cannot change them.
We must use them.

CARDINAL JOHN HENRY NEWMAN

Jesus fell to the ground
and prayed, "My Father,
if it is possible, do not give
me this cup of suffering.
But do what you want,
not what I want."

MATTHEW 26:39, NCV

Any attempt to build our lives
without God is futile and our
labor is in vain. For God is the
Master Builder. Without him,
we can do nothing.

REVEREND ROSALYN GRANT FREDERICK

A young woman constantly complained about her work situation. A friend suggested she was wasting her energy by complaining instead of using her energy to get ahead. "You might not be able to control your bosses," the friend counseled, "but you can change your attitude about them. Changing an attitude can often change the outcome of life."

That we may not complain
of what is, let us see God's
hand in all events;
and, that we may not be
afraid of what shall be,
let us see all events
in God's hand.

MATTHEW HENRY

For God gives wisdom
and knowledge and
joy to a man who is
good in His sight.

ECCLESIASTES 2:26, NKJV

Abiding in him is not a work
that we have to do as the condition
for enjoying his salvation, but
a consenting to let him do all for us,
and in us, and through us. . . .
Our part is simply to yield,
to trust, and to wait for what
he has engaged to perform.

ANDREW MURRAY

Make up for your lack of
ability by abundant continuance
in well-doing, and your
life-work will not be trivial.
The repetition of small efforts
will accomplish more than the
occasional use of great talents.

CHARLES SPURGEON

One needs a will stubborn
in conflict, but apt always
to the total acceptance
of every consequence
of living and dying.

MORRIS L. WEST

Everything is needful
that He sends,
Nothing is needful
that He withholds.

JOHN NEWTON

For thus says the Lord GOD,
the Holy One of Israel:
"In returning and rest
you shall be saved;
In quietness and confidence
shall be your strength."

ISAIAH 30:15, NKJV

The Strength of Courage

Dare to be a Daniel,
Dare to stand alone!
Dare to have a purpose firm!
Dare to make it known!

PHILIP P. BLISS,
Hymn

When circumstances are against us, we must be able to set the sails of our souls and use even adverse winds. The Christian faith does not offer exemption from sorrow and pain and frustration—it offers the power, not merely to bear, but to use these adversities. . . . When you have learned that, you are unbeatable and unbreakable.

E. STANLEY JONES

I am convinced that,
as a child of God,
I am called to risk....
Without risk there
is no opportunity
for personal growth.

RUTH SENTER

Do not fear, for I am with you;
Do not anxiously look
about you, for I am your God.
I will strengthen you,
surely I will help you,
Surely I will uphold you with
My righteous right hand.

ISAIAH 41:10, NASB

Late one evening a small boy
walked along a foggy lane with
his father. Yet the boy did not feel
disquieted. His father was with him;
his father knew the way.

So, too, your Heavenly Father
knows the road of life you tread.
Do not fear; take courage!
Your Heavenly Father is with you;
and He has walked this way before.

It is the end
that crowns us,
not the fight.

ROBERT HERRICK

Great and generous
souls are animated
by opposition and
take pleasure in
breaking through it.

MATTHEW HENRY

What seems unpossessable,
I can possess. What seems
unfathomable, I can fathom.
What is unutterable, I can utter.
Because I can pray. I can
communicate. How do people
endure anything on earth if
they cannot have God?

THOMAS DOOLEY

Be on guard.
Stand true to
what you believe.
Be courageous.
Be strong.

1 CORINTHIANS 16:13, (NLT)

Fear not, I am with thee,
O be not dismayed,
For I am thy God,
I will still give thee aid;
I'll strengthen thee, help thee,
and cause thee to stand,
Upheld by My gracious,
omnipotent hand.

RIPPON,
K in *Selection of Hymns*

No matter how great the
trouble or how dark the outlook,
a quick lifting of the heart
to God in a moment of real
actual faith in him will completely
alter any situation and turn
the darkness of midnight
into glorious sunrise.

MRS. CHARLES E. COWMAN

Father, hear the prayer we offer:
Not for ease that prayer shall be,
But for strength, that we may ever
Live our lives courageously.

L. MARIA WILLIS

It requires moral
courage to grieve;
it requires religious
courage to rejoice.

SØREN KIERKEGAARD

Be strong, and
let your heart
take courage,
All you who hope
in the LORD.

PSALM 31:24, NASB

If we take what he sends,
and trust him for the
goodness in it, even in
the dark, we shall learn
the meaning of the
secrets of providence.

A. B. SIMPSON

The Assurance
of Wisdom

Wisdom is ofttimes
nearer when we stoop
Than when we soar.

WILLIAM WORDSWORTH

The first step of wisdom
is to recognize falsehood.
That which seems
absurd to this world
is often the height of
wisdom to God.

From where then
does wisdom come?
And where is the place
of understanding? ...
God understands its way,
And He knows its place.

JOB 28:20,23, NKJV

The wise man is also the just,
the pious, the upright, the man
who walks in the way of truth.
The fear of the Lord, which is
the beginning of wisdom, consists
in a complete devotion to God.

OTTO ZOCKLER

Most High, Glorious God,
enlighten the darkness of
my heart and give me, Lord,
a correct faith, a certain hope,
a perfect charity, sense and
knowledge, so that I
may carry out your holy
and true command.

FRANCIS OF ASSISI

We must ever be praying—breathing vertically—if we are to have any wisdom from above.

JONI EARECKSON TADA

O Word of God incarnate,
O Wisdom from on high,
O Truth unchanged, unchanging,
O Light of our dark sky;
We praise Thee for the radiance
That from the hallowed page,
A lantern to our footsteps,
Shines on from age to age.

WILLIAM WALSHAM HOW,
Hymn

If any of you lacks wisdom,
let him ask of God,
who gives to all liberally
and without reproach,
and it will be given to him.

JAMES 1:5, NKJV

Paths chosen for us by God
all lead onward and upward,
even when they seem to us to turn
about in inextricable confusion,
and to move downward to the
valleys of humiliation and suffering.
He is the All-Wise, and to him,
wisdom is the way by which
Love gains his victory.

G. CAMPBELL MORGAN

Common sense suits itself
to the ways of the world;
wisdom tries to conform
to the ways of heaven.

JOSEPH JOUBERT

The road to wisdom?
Well, it's plain
And simple to express:
Err
And err
And err again
But less
And less
And less.

PIET HEIN

For the LORD
gives wisdom, and
from his mouth
come knowledge and
understanding.

PROVERBS 2:6, NIV

The Certainty
of Change

God's children do not know
what the future holds, but they
know the One who holds the future,
and in whose hands reposes all
power in heaven and in earth.

WALTER B. KNIGHT

When we resist change or hold onto the past, we only postpone new blessings God has in store for us.

Nothing endures but change.

HERACLITUS

To every thing there
is a season, and a time
to every purpose
under the heaven.

ECCLESIASTES 3:1, KJV

Once in Persia reigned a king
Who upon his signet ring
Graved a maxim true and wise,
Which if held before the eyes
Gave him counsel at a glance
Fit for every change and chance.
Solemn words, and these are they:
"Even this shall pass away."

THEODORE TILTON

We change schools, careers, homes, relationships, and "images" almost as casually as our great-grandparents changed horses. . . . In the kaleidoscopic whirl of our life patterns, it can be enormously reassuring to remind ourselves that God is unchanging: "I the LORD do not change" (Malachi 3:6, NIV).

GINI ANDREWS

Before engraving a granite tombstone, stonecutters spray the stone surface with a rubber coating, stenciling the inscription onto the rubber and cutting that away to expose the stone surface. A sandblaster then cuts across the face of the granite, etching the exposed surfaces. The areas covered with rubber are unaffected by the harsh blasts. . . .

Stonecutters know that rubber is resilient. It will absorb the shock of sandblasting. Our lives, too, can be as hard as granite and blasted to bits by the unexpected. Or, we can be as resilient as rubber that bounces back from life's changes by remaining flexible and going with the flow. The choice is ours!

When times are
good, be happy;
but when times are
bad, consider:
God has made the one
as well as the other.

ECCLESIASTES 7:14, NIV

There is not a heart but has
its moments of longing,
yearning for something better,
nobler, holier than it knows now.

HENRY WARD BEECHER

True faith will
trust God where it
cannot trace Him.

THOMAS WATSON

I make the most of all that comes,
And the least of all that goes.

SARAH TEASDALE

When it is not *necessary*
to change, it is necessary
not to change.

LUCIUS CARY

Notice the way God does things;
then fall into line.
Don't fight the ways of God,
for who can straighten out
what he has made crooked?

ECCLESIASTES 7:13, (NLT)

If the Lord be with us,
we have no cause of fear.
His eye is upon us, His arm over us,
His ear open to our prayer—
His grace sufficient,
His promise unchangeable.

JOHN NEWTON

Photo Credits